Eidolon

Sandeep Parmar

Eidolon

Shearsman Books

First published in the United Kingdom in 2015 by
Shearsman Books
50 Westons Hill Drive
Emersons Green
Bristol
BS16 7DF

Shearsman Books Ltd Registered Office
30–31 St. James Place, Mangotsfield, Bristol BS16 9JB
(this address not for correspondence)

www.shearsman.com

ISBN 978-1-84861-392-8

ACKNOWLEDGEMENTS
Sections of *Eidolon* have appeared or are due to appear in *The Common, Fulcrum, The Other Room Anthology, Poetry International* and *Recours du Poème*.

The Afterword is a revised version of a talk delivered at Queen Mary University—
I am grateful to Hetta Howes and the Department of English for inviting me.
Thanks are due to my family for the long journey from Nottingham to Troy.

This book is for James Byrne,
who gave me the courage.

'The earth may glide diaphanous to death;
But if I lift my arms it is to bend
To you who turned away once, Helen, knowing
The press of troubled hands, too alternate
With steel and soil to hold you endlessly.
I meet you, therefore, in that eventual flame
You found in final chains, no captive then—
Beyond their million brittle, bloodshot eyes;
White, through white cities passed on to assume
That world which comes to each of us alone.'

—Hart Crane, 'For the Marriage of Faustus and Helen'

i.

It was not me, but a phantom
whose oath
    a variable star
mouldering in the reliquary
    is doubt.

    I have not unsealed love, its taproot
        mouthing blackness
        nor seized the fairer woman
to purge from her her song—

    This hell-house of primogeniture, bookish
        and pale   *quartering what is also*
    its own and only rule
        this: fire
and the fire that comes   *from fire.*

ii.

Helen, dispirited
        camera-bound   Helen
fetching the paper from the front lawn in her dressing gown a lot of the time
        and knowing when the phone will ring
        seconds before   by the click of its current

Demi-goddess—not woman, not god
        disembodied like a bowl turned over and its loaf thumping out
                Helen
Queen of never-mind-the-time, of *you can't run on gin for all the everlasting*
        And such

        moths, broiling airlessly in a sodium bulb
                smell of it on her front porch
                        lights on   home

iii.

Waking to a November morning
      to pins running across a yardage of wool
or headaches   the circular world
    disfigured
    by food
          corn cobs in the sink gleam like teeth up her spine
Hurry up the bus goes
and its déshabillement goes   loaming on after it

iv.

I do not insist   *that we retain the old names*
   I would   *know you*

   ever, light   *as the seed*

v.

Marketing the daylong   détente   for a sliver of profit
    does not appear   to bother the kingdom of saints

Ascetics her brothers—
    Spartans   whose only god is [insert here
the death of eleven days]

        Wash the man by the road who turns
          and seeing or not seeing
            is soundless, animal
              wash him
        he is your brother
  enter his encampment (of fuel-scarred fabrics)
        and listen to his black pronouncements
            void of exhaust
      scramble up
  the highway's escarpment
        inviolate, good
          wash him
            or
    be without   brothers

vi.

Helen denuded   Helen
        a place of palor where
        silk shrinks around her throat
        exits   the office

        mindless purposeless walking
        into and out of
        through and over
        up and around
        into and out of
        hands waving mindless purpose

metal tint to everything   Stesichoros blinded
        for watching her
        cross the street
        outside and into
        the car, horn blaring

vii.

<u>U.S. National Interests</u>: Matters of vital interest to the United States to include national security, public safety, national economic security, the safe and reliable functioning of "critical infrastructure", and the availability of "key resources". [*PPD (Presidential Policy Directive) 20*, Top Secret]

It has of course occurred to me   *that this conversation*
        is being recorded   *but what you say*
            does not anyway   *belong to me*

viii.

We are going—shall we go—let us go
and if we do go, knowing little of *where*,
who will put the lamp out as we leave?

(But where is what I started for so long ago?
And why is it yet unfound?) [Whitman]

ix.

Tippeted old Colonial—
Uncle, his mustard handkerchief
like a standard raised to his lips
asks: 'If it's England vs. India
at the Cricket where do you stand?'

In that unholy ditchwell
where there is no victory:
attrition warfare.

'You don't need to know the rules' he sighs,
defeated, adjusting his cravat—burgundy,
printed with small pink elephants,
'We Indians, you know, don't hold a grudge'.

     Primogenitor: 16th-century people of the riverbed
         who wove baskets from the long leaves—

if it hadn't been for the British   and their inexorable
     management
          no doubt we'd still be twisting ropes
              along the Silk Road

x.

In her wine-coloured suit
and burgundy shoes
she asks the night manager
to make a *reverse call*
and he is struck
by her poise

In her hand
the receiver becomes   some object
        cut loose

In 1985 she drove away
from the Britannia Range   of the North Shore
whose wealth heaved silently   out to sea
gathered its silver cuff—
        emolliating—
            uncertain of its allegiance

Helen enclosed in a lantern   carried at arm's length
        Helen   sleeping
                but never lifted off the earth

Her father   turbaned
        and dead these many years now
            sings cross-legged   into some luted harmonium

            once we had so much time
            most rare and unseen world

xi.

Fear   testimony
         wrought across a battlefield
her ghost
         speaks not for itself
         from the painful womb
         of reincarnation

What roads and what gates
         we are always standing in how is it
I am so far again from your gate?

xii.

Helen fails
        in Pharos, Indiana

She makes phone calls   and listens to whomever
        is listening

                I thought I'd call you tomorrow
                        but today is just as good

        plugging numbers into the godhead   plug plug

                I'm going to the County Fair
                        thought maybe you'd want to go?
                                the line damp
                                with sweated palms

The church noticeboard in Pharos urges:
'Destination Heaven / Final boarding call'

The motto of the strip mall's
Things with Strings:
'We'll string you up!'

The bank SOSes between pulses
of time (3:40pm) and temperature (89 degrees):
'Donate crayons to a child, 99 cents'. 'A dozen eggs, 99 cents'.

Temper temper
Super Discount Gun Warehouse
Temper temper
at the flea market-cum-mortuary
Big Red Liquors

Mind your
Aladdin Bail Bonds
Temper
Sparta Amateur Boxing Club

The-corporate-coffee-drone aproned in green:
'Free dessert! Real butter—none of those nasty oils—
we're all really excited about this one!'

Helen samples the red apple cobbler
        smugly—
        how will this moment look in her acid portraits?

"a little child shall lead thee"

xiii.

The 1913 local prosecutor training manual warns
      no 'Jews, Negroes, Dagos, Mexicans
      or a member of any minority race on a jury,
      no matter how rich or well-educated.'

The 1986 manual warns against those with 'multiple gold chains'
      or 'free thinkers'.

xiv.

Cybele
        under the mountain

Helen falls between two limits
        is without documents

She takes a cab—black as a Homburg in winter—
        and peels the notes carefully
        from her purse   the hinges rusting shut
                she rolls quiet as water
                down a cool glass
                as a crow at dusk
                walking backwards
                stealing spoons
                from the verandah

        The TV already on (it's never off)
                greets her with a brief message
                from our sponsors

'No more the puzzling hour nor day' [Whitman]

   though I am here

Herodotus   making probable cause
       for leaving me
in this fit of oceans   in a glimmer of the Dardanelles

xvi.

A peck on the cheek does not stir him
        and leaves no trace
                of red cognition

        Revolving gauntlet of gin

why are you home so late?

        I went to the Fair. I tried to call
        but it rang and rang.

The warm air on her like a poisoned memory
        he blinks and sips

xvii.

In a hotel drawer in 1952 next to King James
        a public service message from Conrad Hilton—

'America on its knees:
        not beaten there by the hammer & sickle, but FREELY, INTELLI-
        GENTLY, RESPONSIBLY, CONFIDENTLY, POWERFULLY.
        America now knows it can destroy communism & win the battle
        for peace. We need fear nothing or no one... ...except
        GOD.'

Uncle Sam
        a pitifully silvered Abe Lincoln
        his sinewy hands pray

'World Peace Through International Trade and Travel'

        'before the darkness falls'
        before 'the pestilence'
        and 'the terror that flies by night'

Old Connie must have been a superstitious man
        lone bed in a hive of strangers
                turning out every morning
                        its own wide-eyed Lazarus

Helen misplaced   in a room   blotting her lipstick
        on industrial-quality tissue   Helen making small talk

        'I am a woman of pleasure' [H.D.]

there was no '*sea-enchantment in his eyes*'

xviii.

'Have you tried our spinach croissants before? They're really delicious!'
What you really mean   is that there's a trapdoor somewhere
behind your register
that we've been playing this game so long
it's hardly worthwhile

The headline on today's *New York Times*:
'N.S.A. Said to Search Content of Messages to and from U.S.'

The President on primetime   in an armchair
praising his wife   now there's a trapdoor

'Have you tried our oatmeal cookies before? They're rrrreally delicious!'

xix.

'As a wheel on its axis turns, this book unwitting to itself,
Around the idea of thee'. [Whitman]

Helen of Sparta   of Troy   in Egypt
          of no known address   of no known nationality
                    refugee of no known conflict
                              stateless   without property
                              disappearing under a veil
                                        of treason

xx.

Her father in his dotage   wielded reason like a butcher

As a child   his hands on the heavy barrow
he cried open-mouthed
at labouring so young

Father wishing now to retire   and divide his kingdom
summoned his daughters to court
posturing at the pulpit
and though he would never take hot irons
to their dissident arms
or change the locks
on the temple doors
(as they do with widows)
his daughters could not
lie

xxi.

Helen dethroned   disinherited Helen   at the crossroads of marriage
               what love is given to a woman
                  whose father
                           is the king of the gods?

    Light apple of gold   in the grass   inedible in its beauty

xxii.

'Ever the dim beginning' [Whitman]

    Under the stucco and concrete plaza
        and its supermarket
        an unredeemable question
        before that
        an anxious crop of wheat
              before the wheat   a rainproof dust that accumulated
                  undisturbed over centuries—

    If as Freud suggests   the mind is a ruined city
        oft plundered oft destroyed
                traumatic structure
            then the market is
                a florescent psychosis
                    a tradewinded hurricane
                        grieflessly cruel
                the sadist's solution to world hunger
                in shrink wrap

'Ever the growth, the rounding of the circle'

    Helen in the cash only express line   15 items or less
    Helen carrying donut peaches   ambiguous, filial

        eyes the tabloids

    The blonde man in front calmly points his finger
        at the Mexican attendant
        'apologize for the wait, go on kiss my ass
        I want you to kiss my ass right now buddy
        you hear me you're gonna kiss my ass'

It appears from the cover stories that European monarchs
are breeding
little feudal lords
in swaddling clothes

Helen offers sympathetically to   the boy—
too young to resort
                      to violence—
'I hope someone runs that asshole over in the parking lot'

In the parking lot
        of the hardware store—

Leaning against white sycamores   in the belting heat
        twenty or so men scattered judiciously

This could be a black and white photograph
their faces like those of the suited men
outside a Bowery soup kitchen
during the Great Depression
the surprise wearing off
slow as a hat pulled down low
for the passing cortège

Beat up Toyotas range round tall   loaded with plywood
        that stings her eyes
Formaldehyde   June gloom   in its hot fog
        ashes to ashes

xxiii.

Helen   where are you
and where is your shadow   Helen
circling the horse
packed with soldiers
war-weary
taunting them
in the voices
of their wives?

xxiv.

'what good to us is a long life if it is difficult and barren of joys, and if it is so full of misery that we can only welcome death as a deliverer?' [Freud]

He is convinced always   looking at his dinner plate
          that somehow he is being cheated

          he examines his wife's face   in this way also
what fair arrangement   of pork and runner beans
          of eyes, nose and mouth
                    would satisfy the white lie of its presentation?

I'd like to go dancing. I'd like to go on vacation.

He rests his fork and knife   watches with a wish her gradual anguish

xxv.

Helen is   instrumental

Laws permit me to refuse your advances
although I have eaten the salt from your table

        As for your hospitality—
I like it anywhere just fine
                so long as I'm coming or going

Helen   is not all but
        scattered like grain

        Vituperate   ghost meaning

        to greet herself   to make room
                for herself   at the table

        to eat a meal of dry meat and vinegar

        Helen is not vital

xxvi.

Blue moon
Full Sturgeon Moon
Full Red Moon
Green Corn Moon
Grain Moon

     dredged up at midnight over Delos
          a colossus in pieces   wellspring of phalluses
             glittering rock of the amphitheatre
               barium and silver
               chist and marble

The Switzerland of pre-history   of the winding Cyclades
     sacred site of unholy sale and savage trade
          Las Vegas meets Versailles
              in the mouths of lions

Delos meaning 'visible'
     pulled like a sequined rug into an adjoining room
          by the arms of Poseidon
             so that Apollo could be born

             [his twin sister Artemis   an afterthought]

Blotted out moon   for the dark purpose   of making bastards into gods

Delos like hot white phosphorus

     so holy even invading armies asked to be blessed as they passed

xxvii.

Helen polyvalent   Helen in a range of other destinies
         traded at port   the port—its own fate

a cradle of violence   a will towards sanctuary   pirated Helen
         illuminated transcript
         of the gossip
                   round the twin marble fountains of the agora

xxviii.

If she ran out of wisdom she does not think
       she would turn to god

                      It would be false
      to follow those inimical visions, contrarily
      feeding on the dark
          Man's mind   in all its weakness
      she notes
      makes itself too available to the churchurring tongues
      of the olive grove   to the rapacity of white-haired prophets

The sun daily makes its dayhop over the crops and that is all

xxix.

Helen   on a coffee date   clandestine
          trading star signs   is a prelude to
                              astrological reassignment

          eavesdropping mothers of small children   black hands
          not really black but pious
                    made for marking out ash crosses
                    or lamenting scorched land

          Mothers   terrible and unpredictable as the sea

Helen is a Virgo
                    Impressed by this her date contends
                    he is both fire and water

xxx.

I am not the virgin mother   *lamenting in the hills above Ephesus*

I am the invective   *injuring these dry plains studded with stone pines*

I am the lateral commemorate   *of war*
    as the steps up to my hiding place suggest
      I am the birther of sacrifice   *received back into*
      the earth   *heavenly rockface*

    if you knew my real name   *you would not*
      use it so lightly

xxxi.

Helen indivisible   in the yellow roar of a crop duster
    she watches it yield and pitch its pitiless circle

    The quickening jumping corroborating schoolchildren
        they circle, too, as if in a dance that honours the gods
        by the lightness of its chaos

        That the field should be fertile with their laughter
          as the outriggers of war pitch and move in
        a merciless circle

xxxii.

An idea is not a woman   but many women
          the composite of an idea

Ours is an older civilization   re-made
          dramatis personae   recast by different troupes
               rebuilt in the style
               of Ionian capitals
               and fluted pilasters
          put through the ringer of the magisterium

                    we see the *real* Helen
                    is the false *we*
                    is the eidolon

xxxiii.

Four US warships   slink up from the coast of the Maghreb
               toward Minoan waters
their sleepless crew tally their charges
as did the Achaeans   counting in each the death of how many

What historical irony
is the citizens of Tel Aviv
buying gas masks
irony itself a mask
for tragedy

xxxiv.

Studio lights singe her chestnut plait of hair—

Today's topic:
'So your husband sacrificed your only daughter that he might win the
war for his brother's wife'

Clytemnestra, what would you say if Agamemnon was sitting here right now?
—The Herald this morning brings chilling news that Troy burns like a
triumphal torch.
And could you find it in your heart to forgive him?
—Never.

The unanimous gasp across the audience of middle-aged women is Helen

xxxv.

Tiresias, in all matters sacred you are ever-present
          as the eunuch in rites of fertility
virile only in speech
you cut a waifish glance
at the cameras
escorted before the Assembly
to receive due punishment

demoted with dishonour   you announce
your intention to live
as a woman in prison
how fitting   to be turned out of the world of men

the andron shuts in
          its flash of medals

Tiresias, the scrolls in the library
cannot be burned
by the invading Goths
          like papyri endlessly scrolling down and up
          invisible   electric

For everything its frame   to each an accordance with its own laws

Codex suggests an end (a teleology?)
but here we are   you say
in the age of immortal beauty

          where no more classified secrets
          or unrecorded moments
          lie in the destruction layer
          of pottery and bones

xxxvi.

Helen in Linear B
at Walgreens

     PA
MA   KA (pharmacy)

tabloids chewing gum energy drinks the 24 hour relief of *Better Homes and Gardens*

    one box of *Nice and Easy* whooshes like a field of rushes
      incarnate welter of thorns that is age

  Helen wishing to conceal her roots   after all   so much colour
    will be wasted on her image   and the slurs on the walls
      of the Roman baths will never anyway call her 'old and grey'

xxxvii.

You are wild-eyed
You are Helen

The grey-blue dawn
the Rosy-fingered Dawn
turning the snaking cloud
into the body of a goddess
raising her thin spear

we glide across
the blue-eyed morning
changing flags
as a woman changes
her lover as often
as another
lover permits
we glide across
zones of conflict

The wind lays down a road
across the waves
hiding us in a mooring of fog
flanks of earth lighten
like fantasy   like Leda's body
to make way for our white ship
of a hundred tiers
and some thousand men

This parthenous soup
of buried cities
held close   we make out

the scent of their joints
the only real thing
in an invented eschatology
of free will

Did I mention the Indiana corn
from whence I came
and its hot unendingness?

       Proud like crosses on a prairie landscape.
Corn madness
industrial corn a devil
bleating like a harp
made of 22 carat gold
High Fructose Syrup
infantile mass delusion   god
sugar fix of empire

Helen makes out the morning freeze
in the stillness of a suspended harvest
what eviction has nature made
in retaliation for these unkillable crops?
Out out for the outing acres of frozen heads.

xxxviii.

I thought you might want to go out, you know, see a bit of life?

If she could be patient enough to wait for his refusal
        (and she is not)
she would hear the air fly out of his lungs
        as she slammed the door shut
            and walked out
                in spite of the hoar frost
                        bending the lawn grass into the usual questions

xxxix.

What is intimacy
    closing and closing again the limits
    of her blouse, her skirt
        barrening the earth with her very existence
          like the angry mother whose child
            is raped in the cavernous underworld
              whose rage burns clear down to the bedrock
              who must still gladden for six months
            of every year

I carry no seed and I know that this, too, effaces me

xl.

'Good morning, how may I direct your call?'

    Good morning
                blight
    Good morning
                blackest coals of mourning
                hard in the infinite   wailing
    Good Night
                to the shaved heads of my kinfolk

I will come to you even if my both hands are in blood
       if the sky is raining knives…

xli.

Helen in media res

    Helen hauling an urn across a battlefield
                        for no apparent reason

    so illogical is the picture   of our deformed antiquity

    the minutes of her day like bared daggers adorned
    with emerald and agate
          so as to distract from their purpose: murder
          slow, fickle

Helen goes out for an hour's lunch
                        the wafts come off her skin
                        desperate, sudden, delicate
                        like an amphora of golden oil
                        a great clay pithos of myrrh
                        slinking across as cargo
                        in a Hittite cosmogony
                        of capital

xlii.

What the neighbours must think of him
    always in his predictable chair
        unless he is shouting at which point he is roused
            to standing and to this day they do not know his name
                Manny Murray M—?

xliii.

'Good morning   good morning   good afternoon'

    Lit up a discalceated simile for time

   Helen
        So lawless in fact   the fact of her
                          is lawlessness

She whose memory pierces eternity
    with its long long needle

xliv.

—You look worried

[Helen] *I'm worried this isn't going to work*

[The elder woman rises, takes a framed certificate off the office wall and hands it to Helen]

—My PhD in Psychoanalysis

[Helen hands it back]

[Helen] *I am to blame for everything*

—you don't really think that—

[Helen] *how do you know?*

—when people lie they curl their toes.

[…]

—how do you feel when he says that?

[Helen] *twenty ways of obliterating myself suddenly come to mind—each uniquely thrilling*

—how can you be to blame for everything?

[…]

—you know pity isn't the same thing as love

I love him too

xlv.

'Some beauty, yes, but not more than her tribe
Lathe-made for stock embraces on a bed.' [Durrell]

Her face erupts in *Hello!* magazine
    how confusing is the testimony
        to her beauty
        for she is no more living
        than Helen—

A little cold, a little dumb, a little worn down by the machinery of love—

'I am astonished when they talk of her [...] this insipid drone!' [Durrell]

If, gilded as a queen, Helen was dragged by her golden hair
    onto Argive ships to be judged by the widows of those who fell
        or blown off course with Paris   to be subsumed by middle age
          on the banks of the merciless Nile
        her defence was always more or less
        noisily offered   on her knees   arms   braceleted hands
          enrapt to beauty

'One tear [...] on the sarcastic cheek'   drawn from the coffers—
             for you to keep
             commemorative souvenir
             of the royal bedchamber

We will judge you by your beauty—we starved aggrieved wide-eyed captives

'Beauty has no obvious use' [Freud]

xlvi.

'Put first before the rest as light for all and entrance-song of all,
That of eidolons.' [Whitman]

No one alive
remembers
the unrecordable
warmth of my
breath

xlvii.

So persistent these abduction fantasies!
Clytemnestra herself would have wept
to know armies would not be raised
for her daughter as for her bitch sister

    The Greeks slipping from her blood
    to the bloodletting of distant altars

    no one would recall her child
turning from a window
eyes burnished like firey opals
    by an ignominious secret love

It was not me—but an image conjured by the mind grieving

Go back to your guilty lives
    savage men, hauling god before his maker

xlviii.

I am the twins   Castor and Pollux
protectors of Helen   or of her astral double
we ourselves   doubled in the heavens
as fate would have it   parted not even in death
strange coinage   to be translated
across so many   master narratives
as inseparable   from one self

Go traveller   *before the wind catches up with your ashes*

xlix.

Let us be as a city upon a hill
    as a stone or several stones
    as white shells in each city's layer
        —each layer a memorable human hour—
            gathering the sea and all its warble in the dust.

If you roll into LA from the East
by car   by road through oaks and sycamores
that give way to studio lots
    barred up like penitentiaries
        dreams assembled stone by stone
        behind a forbidding wall wreathed by wire

If you enter from the air
descending through smog   its brown meniscus
watch the city light up
    like a motherboard on high alert
    from the dry sanctuary between Vegas and mountain ranges
The bric-à-brac of cacti   the desert lore of cannibalism
and invisible tribes of off-the-gridsmen
rattling tinnily in the ears   of cascading Sierras

Let us be as a city
    on the stones of other cities

Troy dignified and silent
    draws a stratified cloak of nine kingdoms
    over its brittle shoulders
Its cape of stone   has been smoothed by the humble footfall
of its slaves and women.

Stop and listen
as you stand high on its brow   hear the hot wind
        rush up the hillsides of brush
through some sort of oak (we think).

We collect its seeds
to plant a Troy-tree
in our Californian garden.
        [My mother, convinced it will live.
Unlike the pomegranate, fruitless, wanting
some eternal myth denied by the Pacific.
Biblical fruit, sole comfort of the dead, its globules of ruby life—
613 cells of blood that pour
in the Babylonian crush
of idle days and endless cruelties,
no, it will not grow on my mother's lawn
in an exile's confusion of lavender,
red marigold and lily flower.]

Mother, let us be as a city, rising
        not swept through
                by the greed of rumoured enemies.

If you arrive by boat to Troy
through quietest midnight   in the pre-blue of black
        slipping in the tide past Lemnos
abrupt on the horizon
you will see the sun erupt
from behind a panorama of cloud

lighted scenes of warring gods
        burning in their silhouettes
                the carnage that burnishes gold
                        scattered without excessive
                                note over the Trojan plain.

1.

Helen as a beam of moonlight   caught sideways
    Helen   refracted onto thresholds   her reflection a holy cult
          of high-born women ululating in bedrooms
              gripping the mirror hard that bears her standard   Helen

'With beauty like a tightened bow'

        The window clapping shut like an iron gate.
        She does the latch. Empty, diffuse glow.

Now focus on her lithe and loathed silhouette
        see if it makes plain
                            how a woman could be mistaken
by so many men   for a ghost   bartered dead by nudest song

                        even in this unacknowledged light
                            at this impossible angle

Afterword: 'Under Helen's Breath'

Some weeks ago, I found myself recounting the impetus for *Eidolon*, the book I had just finished writing, to a fellow poet. I hoped perhaps to set a course in my own mind from the poem's disparate beginnings: Walt Whitman's poem 'Eidolons', H.D.'s *Helen in Egypt*, Euripides' tragedies *The Trojan Women* and *Helen*, as well as a chance opportunity to travel for a week by luxury ship from the Athenian port of Piraeus via the Cycladic islands up through the Dardanelles to the plains of Troy. My explanations spread their purple robes of a self-imposed exile onto a hazily understood vision of antiquity. I can offer no apology for this, except to say that a certain degree of omission has interceded in the place of an ignorance and it is this ignorance of Greek language, of a pure cultural understanding, that is at the heart of the rewriting of Helen from the 8th century B.C.E. to our own century. Virginia Woolf makes the point in her essay 'On Not Knowing Greek' (in which she incidentally transcribes untranslated quotations from Ancient Greek nearly ten times, assuming her reader would follow her understanding of context and linguistic nuance) Woolf argues here that it is impossible to really *know* Greek, language/culture/character, because it is an impersonal literature that is so far removed from the English personality and gesture as to lie flat in a one-dimensional past.

Woolf's point is that we essentially cannot *know* the Greeks because we are so culturally different and their age was not one of aesthetic 'schools' or developmental phases but one that was somehow locked crystalline into a monolithic antiquity. I find this puzzling though not surprising, as Woolf draws from a range of Athenian dramatists, Sophists, lyricists and indeed the epic tradition for evidence that the past did not differentiate itself as does more recent history, for, in her age, archaeological digs—or lootings—were not so advanced that one could be forgiven for seeing antiquity as being one continuous and inseparable moment. So what is the usefulness of the Greeks, whose authorial identities are unfixable, impersonal, whose characters are dictated not by will but by divine fate, whose culture and context are (as the American poet James Merrill writes in his poem 'Lost in Translation') lost like the shade and fibre, the milk and memory of a self-effacing tree? Woolf ends her essay thus: 'With the sound of the sea in their ears, vines, meadows, rivulets about them, [the Greeks] are even more aware than we are of a ruthless fate. There is a sadness at the back of life which they do not attempt to mitigate. Entirely aware of their own standing in the shadow, and yet alive to every tremor and gleam of existence, there they endure, and it is to the Greeks that we turn when we are sick of vagueness, of the confusion, of the Christianity and its consolations, of our own age.'

As I recounted my admiration of Walt Whitman's little-commented-on poem from *Leaves of Grass*, 'Eidolons', I was faced with knowing full well that Whitman's poem is doing what Woolf implies in her essay: to avoid consolation in welcoming the future and to know that every future rises as a ghost of the past, caring little for the lives of individuals, satisfying a whole picture only. Whitman writes '...ever the permanent life of life, / Eidolons, eidolons.' The eidolon, in Whitman's poem, is the enduring shadow into which life is subsumed *and* the force from which life springs eternal. Heavily influenced by his reading of *The Unseen Universe* (1886) by B. Stewart and P.G. Tait, a meditation on the spiritual oneness of all life and the tagline for which is 'the things which are seen are temporal, but the things which are not seen are eternal', Whitman's poem both celebrates and challenges the new birth of America—an industrial nation of giant, even mythic, proportions. Whitman's poem is not altogether successful. Is it too grand. It is too vague. It is not a poem made of words and voices but a poem about an idea and ideas in poems are doomed to fail without the necessary structure around them, which is as often silence as it is the precious din of prophetic statements and the aspirations of genius. Even still, the idea of an eidolon is something beauteous and beguiling. And the eidolon as a *thing* or more correctly as a *preoccupation* is the siren song to the poet who listens for silence.

An Eidolon is an image, a ghost, a spectre, a scapegoat. It is a device, like a *deus ex machina*, to deal with the problem of narrative. One useful example of an eidolon appearing in antiquity is the rising spirit of Patroklos, the beloved friend and warrior loyal to Achilles in the *Iliad*. Poor Patroklos, depicted as a shadowy version of his former glory, hovers expectantly and even impatiently over his tomb as Achilles busies himself with defacing the Trojan prince Hector's corpse. Patroklos tells us more about Achilles than anything—his very existence is as foil to the more famous man and his death precipitates some of the most turbulent and jaw-dropping scenes of Homer's epic. Patroklos was born to die—and to remain unmourned while his friend committed the most egregious atrocities in the name of his unrepentant grief. His eidolon hangs as a warning and as a reminder of the nature of the superior Myrmidons and all the united tribes of the Greek isles. However, sent to Troy on an ill-advised mission, the Greeks are lured into aggression by the most cunning and enduring eidolon of all—at the centre of the *Iliad* is Helen's spirit-double. Now there are several versions of Helen's fate and several differing views of the cause of her elopement to Paris, starting of course with the apple of discord and culminating in a ship chase to Asia Minor sometime in the 11th century B.C.E. What Hilda Doolittle, the modernist poet, clings to is the Helen/eidolon best celebrated by Euripides' 5th-century tragedy simply entitled *Helen* and his theory of Helen's fate is essentially this: that, when Helen and Paris left Sparta for Troy on one of his ships, it was blown off course and landed in Egypt. There, Helen was kept by the Egyptian King as captive and Paris was sent back home to Troy empty-handed. Ten years pass of a tiresome war—all in the name of returning Helen to her now (rather angry) betrayed husband Menelaus. And the rest, wooden horse and all, we know. The blamed woman, the by now quite hated woman (by Greek heroes, by Greek citizens, and especially by the heroes' wives who strongly object to their husbands being carried off by such a false purpose as a Queen's infidelity) Helen is redeemed by the simple replacement of the real flesh-and-blood Helen for the image/ghost who vanishes into thin air at the war's end. Paris is followed back to Troy by Helen's eidolon, who is portrayed brilliantly by the 20th-century German writer Christa Wolf in the novel *Cassandra* as a chiffon-thin shadow of woe.

I found myself falling under the trance of this false Helen and wondering where the real Helen really was and if her existence even mattered. Probably it does not. Helen has been passed down to us in the guise of more than just a very bad woman: she is a machine, she is a murderer of heroes, she is a faithless woman, she is, as Bettany Hughes puts it bluntly in her exhaustive historical study of Helen, a 'Goddess, Princess, Whore.' She seems to me the perfect teleological argument for the irrelevance of women's narrative agency. This must be of course why H.D. was so drawn to her, but also why Helen of Troy, or Helen of Sparta, depending on your bias, has not lost any appeal in the nearly three thousand years of her history. Whenever Helen speaks from within a text (or even in the same text sometimes) it is through a *different* voice—not like the Greek gods whose iconography is more or less stable, knowable and often noble. Helen is identified (not unusually) by her ancestry: her father (Zeus and Tyndareus alike) and mother (Leda), the strange and violent circumstance of her birth (born of rape by a god), Helen's own rape by King Theseus whilst she was an adolescent, and of course her eventual marriage to Menelaus after a grand contest of suitors and her subsequent affair with Paris. There are countless sources over thousands of years that mark Helen's evil nature—and her extraordinary beauty. The cruelty of both seem to go hand in hand. The *Encomium of Helen* by the 5th-century Sophist and rhetorician Gorgias, is a rare defence of Helen and a reprieve from blame for causing the devastating Trojan War. But the *Encomium* is also a trick—a defence of rhetorical manipulation (one probable cause for Helen's elopement) by employing the very manner by which Helen was convinced to leave home and family and kingdom to go to Troy with Paris. Men trained in rhetoric or lyrical skill care to make little defence of Helen, unwieldy and indescribable as she is beyond being beautiful and unusually blondish or red-haired. The preserving of Helen's image relies on a much enjoyed perversion of her image—and only the eidolon, granted to her from a couple of ancient sources but most fully by Euripides, allows her to escape the tragic error of her lust.

I take my cue, if you like, from Helen's multiple forms and her indefensible silences and it is my primary interest to re-interpret Helen for a new age, with new concerns and new fearful eidolons of false value and worthless commodity. Just as the tragedians of antiquity transmuted concerns of their day into mythological structures, it is my hope to demonstrate the spectral nature of unrecorded or suppressed narratives, scapegoated for the greater purposes of citizenry, nation-building and global dominance. Of all the great scenes and speeches in tragedies performed in classical antiquity, by far the most poignant and fitting for my purposes is the god Poseidon's lament just after the fall of Troy, the city of his patronage. Facing a smouldering ruin, Poseidon recounts the story so well known of the city's fall to an assembled audience (the gods speak! they touch the ground! they grieve!) and he details what is to come immediately in the action of the play. The most piteous widows and mothers of Troy's heroes (Hector, Priam, Paris), who have scratched their faces with their fingernails and torn their hair out of their skulls and are ravaged by madness, are to be divvied up by the senior Greek warriors to become the slaves of the men that killed their husbands, brothers, sons. Poseidon judges the scene thus by saying: 'now I must leave / Ilion the famous, leave my altars. When desolation / Falls like a blight, the day for the worship of gods is past.' Abandoned as these women are and made into the spoils of war, heaped onto ships weighted with Trojan loot, even the gods are forced to turn away. This put me in mind of the oft-quoted line from Derek Walcott's poem, 'Sea Grapes': 'the Classics can console, but not enough'. Can we afford to read the enslavement of women by the noble Greeks so detachedly? Can we model, as we have, a civilization on one that exploits, ensnares and silences women, the more 'advanced' it becomes? Where women are traded as prizes and their narratives of 'goddess, princess, whore' are determined not by any will or intent but by the wholesale utility of their being apportioned with blame? If the Trojan war was not about 'the face that launched a thousand ships', then it was about secure and much sought-after access to trade routes into Asia from the Mediterranean, regional dominance, strategic placement in the path of invading armies from the Middle East, etc, etc, etc. The *Iliad* begins with Achilles and Agamemnon, fighting on the same side, arguing over a slave girl, Briseis, brought in to comfort men languishing without their wives for a decade, but these men could just as easily be arguing over oilfields, gas pipelines, disputed borders, far-flung and well-appointed military bases in Turkey or the Sinai peninsula. No, the classics cannot console because, like modernity, antiquity is a buffed-up version of heroism, passed through many hands and attributed to many consequences; it is a narratological failure and if it is impersonal, as Woolf writes, then this allows for greater violence to take place within the textual choreography.

I promised to tell a story that I'm putting off, on purpose. I began with the phrase—'archival impulse'—and will now endeavour to move away from the monotony of mortals chained to oars in great ships (the injuries of centuries) in order to briefly explore what the archive means to us and to Helen. As Jacques Derrida defined in his now seminal work *Archive Fever*, 'archival violence' is the consigning of texts to an archival unity, a oneness which affirms the unique exemplarity of the author and his work. Derrida wrote, 'As soon as there is the One, there is murder, wounding, transformation... It becomes what it is, the very violence—that it does to itself. Self-determination as violence.' Though in this context Derrida is specifically referring to the 'totalizing assemblage' of a culturally constructed people and the violence that is committed by unifying their individual hopes and motives into 'One', his metaphor expands beyond this into the abuse of the power to consign. Who gives Helen her voice and what need unites it into a single constant loathsome creature? Helen is as much the city of Troy as its famed plains and high walls. It might as well be Helen smouldering on the great pyre of defeat, even though she escapes unscathed in the *Odyssey* and is restored to her husband's side by the eidolon's unique guarantee of Helen's chastity. Worst of all it is Helen's silence—or the silencing of Helen—by epic, tragic, poetic narratives (save Gorgias and Euripides) that makes it difficult to forgive. She makes no attempt to author her story and her keeping *schtum* is a symptom of the archive. After all, we don't make archives of things that have not fallen somehow into obscurity or are in no need of preserving, archives are guided by the principles of silence—the fear of silence, the substantiating of silence, the insertion forcibly of the place where silence ends and begins, and this is to a large extent artificial. Maybe Helen was giving her reasons, sharing from within her cage of incomparable beauty (and its natural correlative—commodity) her side of the story or her refusal to join in the myth-making of Helen 'under her breath'? Poetry relies on the gathering of fragments and is happy to let things lie disconnected but by the box, folder, site of archival consignment in which it exists reluctantly, petulantly, without conclusion. In our modern age, it is easy, perhaps too easy, to imagine that the ghost of Helen is ever-present, rising out of the unmourned grave to offer her warning to those of us busied by violence, greed and the causing of needless suffering. When Allen Ginsberg imagines Whitman as the ferryman Charon, looking back at a MacCarthyite America from the smoking bank of Lethe in the poem 'A Supermarket in California', it's an almost Troy-like image of ruin from which issues the eidolons bound towards oblivion. My poem involves itself necessarily in the formation of discourse around citizenship, national identity, surveillance, consumption, the wizardry of global finance, the din of distant wars. When Euripides wrote *The Trojan Women* Athens had just committed genocide on the Cycladic island of Melos (whose rock face is eerily reddish to this day) and repopulated the rogue state with its own people. The horrifying odour of war dead invoked by the playwright in defiance of Athenian brutality made for an unpopular but timely subject. It is not possible today to follow Helen to Egypt, as H.D. did on a cruise several decades ago. Cairo is a door locked from the inside and then set on fire to end an argument founded on the imperatives of Empire. On the note of government surveillance—I was struck recently by how much material is being archived that has little or no relevance to a narrative purpose, our telephone calls or email subject headings or web searches reveal a totally misconstruable version of ourselves and this, too, is a kind of effacement via a glut of information. The fear was that only after the fact of suspicion or arrest can these records be revisited in order to build an evidential base for the foregone conclusion of guilt. This does not seem so dissimilar to the achrontic violence done to Helen, arch criminal in a labyrinth of beauty offered and beauty withheld. I am interested, too, by the spectral nature of democratic systems, their own labyrinths.

My poet friend—by now probably forgotten as the beginning of my story—listened to my enthusiasm for Greece, its gods, its language and after a brief pause (possibly to draw from some wellspring of doubt deep within, he, like myself an Indian trained in the logic of the West) he asked hotly: 'Why don't you learn Sanskrit? Write about our mythology instead?' He proceeded to tell me that the gods in Europe were long dead and that in India they are still alive, dragged out annually for festivals, ritualized performances, marionettes even, set ablaze as the mortal enemies who live in the imagination of Indian children from the moment they can grasp speech. I was stunned, taken aback really, by the idea that I could not write about the Greeks legitimately because I was the wrong colour, the wrong race, and that any version of Helen I undertook could only ever aspire to an epistemological end—one that puts *our* literature over *their* literature. Like when Macaulay famously wrote in 1835 that 'a single shelf of a good European library was worth the whole native literature of India and Arabia'. The archive's silences opened up and swallowed me as I languished on the edge of failure knowing nothing of the Greek language and deserving nothing of its meanings. I could not, I would not, write about Surpanakha, the female devil from the *Ramayana* who was so hideous in her love of a wandering prince that he cut the nose off her face. Or the long-suffering, pious and chaste Sita, or Drapaudi. Or the goddesses I couldn't keep straight with their monstrous forms and premises. In truth, Hindu culture was as strange to me as Ancient Greece, more so, because I was raised as a Sikh and Sikhs are convinced that Hinduism represents an absurd plurality of variety and superstition like throwing water at the sun to end drought or wives annually fasting to extend their husbands' lives. I prefer the monsters of classical myth: the Minotaur, Argos, the Cyclops, Medusa, Scylla. And not knowing Greek at all really beyond translated texts, dutifully studied as foundational to an enjoyment of English literature, not being admitted to a school where Greek was as common as the Mexican Spanish I learned fluently in California, led me to the important conclusion that *what* we write about is as crucial as *what does not* tempt us. Anyway, maybe it is better to write about gods that are dead after all—the living ones are so exacting and demand their likeness be preserved at the expense of the artist.

Whilst doing some archival research at the University Library at Cambridge in the papers of the Reverend Hugh Stewart, I came across something rather extraordinary, something I had not expected to find— you see, my main purpose for Stewart's correspondence was to glean mentions of his friend, the modernist poet Hope Mirrlees. Tucked away, almost imperceptibly signed, was a letter written by the infamous MP Enoch Powell to the Reverend in 1935 whilst Powell was a student at Trinity College. It began simply: 'Dear Dr Stewart, The funeral speech reference is Aristotle Rhet I 7 (superscript 34) = 1365a:' And then there is a long transcription in perfect geometrical symmetry of Ancient Greek, presumably the aforementioned passage though I would struggle to confirm it. I believe I gasped, and then marvelled at the beauty of its surface, of the care this man—a man who would live like a red-eyed demon in my mother's nightmares as a child in Wolverhampton in the late 1960s—his exact script copied out the funeral speech from Aristotle. Enoch Powell's Greek shook with an intelligence that I hated to admit. What happened between 1935 and 1968 when the man stood and imagined he saw the river Tiber foaming with much blood? Was that now famous image the unnatural endpoint of a devoted Classical education? Indeed, what moved him to issue such an edict of race war, to become in one person the culmination of lesser-educated, quieter curses of hate so numerous and so well-known to my mother's generation and to her father, who stood outside his butcher shop in Derby brandishing a meat cleaver, warding away drunken football fans from his shop windows when back in India he had been in an earlier life, of all things, a banker?

Sandeep Parmar

Lightning Source UK Ltd.
Milton Keynes UK
UKHW041324250222
399233UK00002B/66